Translation is a craf
experience of those who l
I am sure that l
Guillemin's book at va   ...careers in
search for the advice of an experienced professional.

Gabriela Widmer, BA, translation project manager, Buenos Aires

Based on his professional knowledge, George is sharing simple but useful tips and tricks for being a passionate freelance translator. His guidelines provide valuable insights for all language industry stakeholders.

Tino Hother, Head of Business Operations,
text&form translation agency, Berlin

These guidelines offer a pragmatic, no-nonsense approach. George is ahead of his game and the wisdom he imparts in the following pages are earnestly worth a read if you are serious about the job you do.

Nick La Faci, proprietor, Rheingau Language School, Geisenheim

For the customer, the freelancer presents a triad of commitment, competence and pricing. If you are (nearly) always on hand and have extra know-how to contribute on occasion, your price will be accepted, as George Guillemin reports in this compelling account of his professional practice: mandatory reading for anyone considering permanent self-employment.

André Schlüter, Ph.D., Senior Communication Consultant,
RUECKERCONSULT, Berlin

George Guillemin

FREELANCE TRANSLATOR

George Guillemin owns and operates the Guillemin Translations agency, which focuses exclusively on the real estate sector. Having read American Literary History in Munich, Santa Cruz/California and Berlin, he obtained a Ph.D. to prove it. Apart from a book of literary criticism, he is the author of several works of prose, poetry and photography. He lives in Berlin and has been self-employed since 2002.

FREELANCE TRANSLATOR

Frontline Guidance

George Guillemin

with a preface by
Silke Lührmann

EDITION CAFÉ DE NUIT

Freelance Translator
George Guillemin
International paperback edition
Berlin: Edition Café de Nuit, 2019
www.edition-cafe-de-nuit.com

ISBN-13: 9781793845603

It's like a lot of things, said the smith. Do the least part of it wrong and ye'd just as well to do it all wrong. ... Reckon you could do it now from watchin? he said.

Do what, said Ballard.

Cormac McCarthy, *Child of God*

Contents

Freelance Translator

Preface

Back in the days when dinosaurs roamed the earth and the digital economy was in its infancy, George and I used to joke about going into business together as "purveyors of fine wordcraft". Things didn't work out that way – if they had, more than likely this book would now contain another cautionary tale about the perils and pitfalls of mixing business with friendship. But having been the beneficiary of George's wisdom and experience for over twenty years, I am delighted that he has decided to share them with a wider audience.

Still, as George reminded me the other day, when he first confessed his intensifying "urge (...) to put pen to paper and theorize on the psychology of translating in my specific field, or to share my Best Practice nuggets" last autumn, my initial response wasn't quite as enthusiastic as it could have been. Instead, I sent him an e-mail that worried about the benefits to bright young novice translators desperate for advice and demanded to know: "Is it just going to be the amusingly idiosyncratic musings of a middle-aged translator dude, or are you actually going to offer anything that might be useful for anyone else?"

The book that dropped into my inbox the other day is most definitely both, or possibly neither. George's account of what it actually feels like, on a day-to-day level, to earn a living at the "wordface" (as Emma Wagner calls it in her dialogue with Andrew Chesterman[1]) of professional translation, is raw, intimate and honest, at times painfully so. It is also laugh-out-loud funny. At a historic moment when many of us are struggling to compete with the speed and rapidly improving fit-for-purpose quality of neural machine translation engines, this could so easily have turned into an elegy for a profession on the brink of economic obsolescence.

Instead, George gives us a compelling 130-page argument for the added value human translators bring to the task: the craftsperson's passionate "desire to do something well for its own sake", as the American sociologist Richard Sennett[2] puts it –

---

[1] *Can Theory Help Translators? A Dialogue Between the Ivory Tower and the Wordface* (London: Routledge, 2002)
[2] *The Culture of the New Capitalism* (New Haven: Yale University Press, 2006)

whether that something is a table that didn't start life as a flat pack from a Nordic home furnishing chain, a cooked-from-scratch lasagne or indeed a well-turned phrase. For Sennett, the craftsman (his use of inclusive pronouns suggests that he does mean women, too) is the opposite of both the "consultant, who swoops in and out but never nests", and the consumer, who "dwell(s) in material desires which die when consummated". While "for the consumer, stimulation lies in the very process of moving on", the craftsperson "digs deep into an activity just to get it right" and takes pride in a job well done. Craftsmanship, Sennett concludes, "represents the most radical challenge" against "the triumph of superficiality at work, in schools, and in politics (...). Perhaps, indeed, revolt against this enfeebled culture will constitute our new fresh page."

If these "nuggets" fall short of offering a one-size-fits-all model for aspiring freelance translators to follow, that's because translators come in all shapes and sizes, and none will ever fit them all. I should know because I've been studying them for the past three years as part of my PhD research into working conditions in the language services market. Time and again, I've been struck by the rich diversity of attitudes and opinions that comes across in my findings – as well as by the extent to which respondents from different backgrounds shared similar experiences and would often use almost identical wording to describe them.

This book adds another rich layer of insight to the data I've already gathered in my current hybrid guise as a scholar-practitioner. In future, whenever I find myself overwhelmed by what George fittingly calls "the relentlessness of it all" – the never-ending rush to meet one tight deadline after another, the conflict between clients' expectations of instant responsiveness and constant availability and the single-minded focus required to do justice to my inner craftsperson's desire to dig deep... – I'll sleep better knowing that I have his "unruly, maverick affair without structure or index" to turn to for guidance and solace.

Finally, as I also pointed out in that less-than-constructive e-mail quoted above: "Hell, I can remember being a desperate bright(ish) young(ish) thing myself!" I would have appreciated these amusingly idiosyncratic musings as much then as my duller older self cherishes them now.

Silke Lührmann, MA, Swansea/Wales
freelance translator and educator

Introduction

"No man is an island," John Donne famously wrote in 1624 and who would dispute his words the way they were meant? Yet the solitary business of being a self-employed translator has very much a Robinson Crusoe feel to it, and no amount of networking will seriously contest the freelancer's status as a sovereign island nation. You may start out working for an agency, possibly in-house even, but as the years progress and with them your degree of specialisation, you watch the cliffs along your shoreline crumble and the bridges burn with a mixture of pride and dread until you realise there is no one left to substitute for you if you were to go on a holiday. Which you won't because you can't.

You like to do your own thing and do it in your own sweet way, feel no obligation to play by the rules, make a poor team player, are loath to call for a life preserver even when out of your depth. Like as not, it is precisely the detachment that comes with the territory (or lack thereof) that makes you good at what you do.

Assuming your island does not get washed away altogether and that your business thrives, you settle in, work long days, fret and strut your hour upon the stage—and suddenly want to be heard. One morning, you find yourself at peace with the mainland, realise that you've become milder, more conciliatory. You may wish to clamber back aboard the ship you jumped and share your tale with the crew, wanting the professional community you left to listen to you now and to approve. Indeed, you may have tired of your solitude and feel the urge to share some hermit wisdom and a word of caution with the would-be renegades you cannot dissuade outright from following your self-marooning footsteps. And then again, perhaps that's just me.

A few years back, someone who knows and likes me thought it a good idea for me to come down for a visit to the translating school where she was enrolled and give a talk on what it's like to be a freelance translator: about the pros and cons of becoming one, the dos and don'ts of being one. She talked to the school's owner and he nodded and made her a cup of Earl Grey, offered to cover the air fare. It was all the prompting I needed, that and the prospect of getting to share what I had learned in my line of work, and simply getting to talk, for it can get quite lonely here in this office. No one ever comes by and rarely do I leave except perhaps to grab a cup of coffee at the Greek's around the corner.

It proved a disaster. I had brought detailed notes for a twenty-minute lecture, pre-prepared answers for questions likely to be asked, xeroxed a sheaf of nifty handouts, but I spent my time rambling until I lost my voice, going off on tangents until it was time to head back to the airport when I had not even covered half of what I had meant to discuss. This book before you now is arguably my second chance to ramble away as I see fit and to cover any tangent that comes to mind. It is an unruly, maverick affair without structure and index, and chances are that things you read here at night will prove impossible to find the next morning. It's not supposed to be a textbook, and it elaborates on neither theory nor method. I love to talk, I love to write, and as I get to do both in abundance, the bric-a-brac of experiences and insights becomes the signature feature of this journal.

Another reason for putting pen to paper is sheer tradition, meaning that any practitioner with a certain number of years on the job will have hands-on advice to share with novice practitioners or even with curious clients who might be keen to make the collaboration with their translators more effective. It is arguably impossible to provide too much frontline coverage from a field whose practice defies standards and convention, and where guidance must necessarily differentiate and take exception in order to remain meaningful in any given context. What works in one sector may be ineffective in another, and what is Best Practice for an agency may compromise the flexibility that is the freelancer's stock in trade.

An obvious advantage of anecdotal evidence is its easy intelligibility, which is why any good textbook illustrates its lessons with examples. Better yet, the anecdotes will work their magic entirely on their own—without abstracting or reaffirming a principle—if you are willing to trust your senses over established procedure. In the often volatile environment of freelance translating, improvised tactics will carry the day more often than long-term strategy, and so a handbook of random observations is arguably par for the discourse.

Thirdly, the ceaseless rain of job applications by fellow translators in my in-box has made me wonder wearily what makes people mail out these hapless pleas without talking to someone or reading something first. And the answer may well be that they have no one to talk to, nothing to read, castaways just washed ashore the isle of self-employment. Neither academia nor an occasional internship provide a failsafe recipe on how to build up a client base, because there is none. While networking is key, an excellent network will not in and of itself generate demand.

During the aforementioned talk at the language school I called it a waste of time to actively solicit your services, and the school's owner cut in and objected nervously, worried that I was making the career prospects of his charges look bleaker than they were. But nothing he said at the time and nothing I have observed since has made me change my mind. While I have no catch-all alternative to offer, you may find some of the suggestions in here helpful in positioning yourself to advantage. One of them would be that shifting the focus from an excellent network to networked excellence is a subtle but decisive difference.

In a word, this is not another how-to manual, but rather a potpourri of empirical jimmies to be sprinkled on the rich fudge sundaes of translation theory and skills. Rather than bypass or indeed disparage the standards of an ancient profession, it seeks to complement them and hone them in a day and age where the one thing saving the freelance translator from C3PO and his electronic ilk is the organic complexity of the human mind.

Translators come in all sorts, and these musings are relevant to commercial translators serving private businesses only. Nothing I say applies to the academic or literary translator. They are a breed of their own, governed by rules without analogue in the clock-paced world. The same goes for certified or government-appointed translators and interpreters: They are on their own. In fact, what I have to say may be irrelevant or wrong outside my field of expertise, which is real estate, or for any but the single language pair I cover, which is English and German. And even if you mine the same specialist vein, you should take all of this with a grain of salt and by no means more seriously than it was intended.

Let me close by saying that there is no point in reading the off-the-cuff miniatures below in sequence or in any other order. Just pick one that grabs you and ponder it for a while after reading it. Skip the ones that bore you. Enter your thoughts and comments into a notebook and do collect your own experiences. Join a blog to compare notes with others or start your own. Share your tales, prattle away. As suggested above, it is hardly possible to have too much first-hand experience in a trade so personal and complex. Don't be the carpenter whose work progressed so slowly due to the dullness of his tools that he found no time to sharpen them. While they tend to be introverts, even and especially freelancers stand to benefit from the dialogue with fellow practitioners. No man is an island, and woman even less so.

Enter the Freelancer

So, what is a freelancer? For the purposes of this book, a freelancer is not a self-employed translator doing agency work. To me, who quit taking agency jobs many years ago, working for one or more translating agencies resembles a form of disenfranchisement with all the drawbacks of being self-employed and none of the benefits. You play by the same rules as permanently employed in-house translators, but without the holidays, without health coverage, without pension plan and without sick leave, to say nothing of parental leave. You work for a pittance that is dictated not by, but to, the agencies in a fiercely competitive buyer's market.

That being said, I advise any rookie translator to start with agency work because there is no better way to familiarise yourself with the routines and workflows, the software and interfaces, the work in a team and with client-side resources. Indeed, you have seen nothing yet as a commercial translator until you have worked on a million-word job in software localisation with several dozen fellow colleagues using a central in-house server, off-site client servers, machine translations, query sheets, mandatory style guides and glossaries, and all of this against a tight deadline. Not least, you get to train on the job while still having someone between you and the client, who has no idea that you are new to this line of work. It is a very useful way to start being self-employed, but there is no freedom to speak of, and so you are not a freelancer by my book.

The type of freelancer I want to talk about represents a third-party service provider who negotiates directly with his or her clients, accepts and completes assignments, does his or her own invoicing and accounting. For the client, this kind of one-man show is basically just another business whose services are available on the open market at prices the vendor quotes, not the buyer. In my case—and no doubt the same goes for the careers of many—it has been a mixed bag of both, learning the ropes from the bottom up in an agency while serving a circle of direct clients at the same time, and using the credentials earned through the agency job to expand the own clientele over time, until one day you feel confident enough to take a deep breath and set up shop for yourself.

As with any trade, a promising way to make a success of it is to have something unique to offer and then to make yourself indispensable by providing it. The freelance translator may do so first of all by specialising in a given field of expertise and secondly by building up a database for each client. While the primary purpose of computer-assisted translation (CAT) is quality assurance, it is also a brilliant customer retention scheme because the discounts you grant on previously translated matches—fully matching sentences—make it prohibitively expensive for the client to switch to another translator.

Serious differences would have to develop or something go wrong badly to make them want to do that. Neatly dovetailing with this, your degree of specialisation should ensure that your clients find few translators to replace you and probably none who are more affordable.

The brilliance of this business model is simultaneously its greatest shortcoming because you, like your client, will find no one to replace you if ever you were to fall ill or plan a holiday. Even if you found someone with your exact skillset, you would have to surrender your database, meaning the one thing that might qualify as the goodwill of your business. You would be risking your livelihood.

You are exposed to the same risk if you hire people or contract their services. Once they have dealt with your clients and understand the nature of your business with them, they may take that business from you, and the risk is very real. Even if they die trying you will lose those clients because trust can be restored no more than a broken vase. I must admit that I have not found a solution to this dilemma yet, and as a result no one works with me or for me at the moment.

There is, however, a third way to make yourself indispensable, and it is the one this book is about, an empathetic approach that I have found to be the most effective because it is tied to you as a person and to the sum of your personal experiences. My hope is that eventually it will ensure that in my absence my clients will simply miss me and my good care even if they are well looked after by employees or partners of mine, and that they will breathe a sigh of relief when I return from my holiday or wherever instead of seducing my staff or partner or letting themselves be seduced by them.

Rather than being a spanking new approach, it may ultimately boil down to professional sensitivity and experience in the traditional sense, and there is a chance that nothing I say here will be news to a veteran in the service sector, but it is a chance I'm willing to take. After all, my intended reader is obviously not the veteran translator who, I am sure, is busy writing his own memoirs at this very moment.

One of the more fat-free takeaways of Zen Buddhism is the so-called ox-herding tale, in which the Zen practitioner in search of his true self first hunts for the ox, then herds him and finally becomes one with him. Apply this meditative exercise to freelance translating and you have the gist of this essay in a nutshell. You may laugh, but let me tell you I am most content with my performance whenever I have managed to "become the client," that is, having succeeded in putting myself in the client's shoes.

In essence, this means becoming sensitive to my clients' needs to the point where I feel safe enough to take liberties with their narratives and abandon set standards of my trade in order to deliver translations they believe are the exact equivalent of their source copy. Nothing gratifies me more as a craftsman than being able to inspire this degree of discursive reassurance in my clients.

Over dinner with friends or on the phone when declining a job, I will occasionally compare myself to a blacksmith who crafts one wrought-iron handrail a day, perhaps two, but no more, and who takes pride in his craftsmanship. He could hire a dozen apprentices and produce two dozen handrails, but it would not be the same. My clients usually get the picture right away and appreciate it, more so than they would if I compared my job to ox-herding. In contradistinction to the work of literary translators, who are artists in their own right, you could probably call this an artisanal approach to freelance translating, but we won't call it anything of the kind, of course, lest we romanticise a rock-solid business.

Let me close with a technical distinction, if only because it keeps amazing me how few people are aware of it: Unless you form a company or partnership, you do not need a business license to be a freelance translator, because you belong in the group of the so-called free professions, together with artists, lawyers, architects, physicians and journalists, among others. At least in Germany (and probably in most European countries), this means you are not limited to commercial premises but may rent a regular flat or just maintain a home office and still get to write it off as a business expense. Many landlords are unaware of this and get nervous, fearing they may have to pay a misappropriation charge for renting residential accommodation to a commercial business.

Also good to know is that, although you are not (the head of) a commercial enterprise, you can and should get your own VAT identification number right away because you are entitled to input tax deduction like a regular business, meaning you get to set off any VAT you paid for business-related expenses against the VAT paid to you by your clients at the end of the same month. Knocking the sales tax off your bills can be a big break especially when you are still in the process of setting up and need to buy all sorts of stuff.

Finally, I highly recommend getting a tax consultant from the start because, on top of knowing things you may not even have considered, you get to file your income tax return six months later than those without a tax consultant, which is helpful when your revenues are growing year on year (again, this reflects the situation in Germany). If you hire help, the tax consultant will also take care of your payroll accounting and employer's insurance, a service many novice freelancers are unaware of. What I personally love most about having a tax consultant is that I never have to deal with the inland revenue office directly. This is more or less all the legal advice you will get in this book, and you might want to put it back on the shelf if you need a "how-to" business manual on regulatory, financial and technical matters.

Sell Yourself Short

From time to time, someone will suggest that I'm selling myself short. Friends who say this mean nothing by it except that they would like me to do well, almost as well as they are doing. They have people working for them, whereas I have not, and it appears to be a difference that counts. It would never occur to friends in permanent employment or self-employed in their own right to suggest anything of the sort. But for the entrepreneur friends it has proven the way to wealth to have people work for them, to host meetings with customers, to attend conferences and trade fairs, to keep winning customers, to move to ever bigger quarters to accommodate their growing number of staff, to upgrade the fleet and all the rest of it. Dynamic growth has been their measure of performance. They are good at what they do, and they believe anyone with a sound business idea and proper resolve can do the same. The unspoken assumption is that everyone subscribes to the same model of success, wants to be like them, and that those who fail to pull it off are selling themselves short.

If I tell my entrepreneur friends I cannot take a given assignment at the moment because I'm booked out they wonder how on earth I could have gotten myself in such a fix. They will ask me why I don't get help, why I don't have five people working for me or twenty-five. Their idea of running my business would be that I handle the front end, do the conferencing and masterminding while some competent worker bees do the actual work at the back-end. Or outsource the whole shebang and concentrate on panache. These amicable, well-meaning go-getters would probably nod enthusiastically at the end of the ox-herding tale in my opening chapter and propose that the seeker go into cattle ranching next.

The other day someone got mad because I declined to take him on as a new client. He had previously managed a certain account at one of my oldest clients, and I had done the translations for that account. Neither this person nor the end client had been easy to work with, and I had felt genuine relief at the idea of having them off my back. But here he was, setting up an agency of his own and assuming I would continue to handle the translating end for that account. He had been patronising then, hard to work with, and the chances of him being less dominant as the head of his own outfit were nil. He became quite impatient when I took a rain check, and he more or less suggested that I was not playing by the rules if I turned down a new account, an up-and-coming firm like his. He told me point blanc there must be something wrong with my business model.

It never occurred to him that I might not be playing his game. That we are playing different games. The thing is, I'm not really running a business, and there is no business model. But I can tell almost instantly whether or not I will get along with a person and whether our collaboration will be harmonious and fruitful. Making a living on your own is never easy, but one of the perks that freelance work does have is that it is entirely up to you to decide who you want to work for. You don't have to explain to anyone why you are not interested in a job, and you cannot be fired either. In this case, it was tempting to be blunt and say

"Sorry, mate, but you and I are on different wavelengths and I just can't work with people like you." But you never know. People change, and so do circumstances. There might come a time when you are desperate for any kind of work, and would accept a job from Beelzebub if he needed a translation. So, I just told him "So sorry, booked solid through the end of the month." He ended the call by offering help (with my business model) if I needed any, and that was kind.

But like I said: This is not really a business, and there is nothing wrong with my business model because I don't have one. It makes no sense to talk about a business model if there are no alternative models to choose from. A freelance journalist accepting or declining assignments would probably not think of the criteria that determine the decision as his or her "business model" either. I used to know an engineer-turned-translator whose brother had built up prospering translation agency and who thought he could do the same. Encouraged by a few big jobs, he hired forty people, and five minutes later the jobs stopped coming, or so it seemed, and you can imagine the rest. Fellow translators who worked for him still talk about his folly. The market is awash with translators, and there is always someone who will do it for less, always. I know agencies that wax and wane like the moon, paced by the whims of their big-ticket clients. I myself was bold enough to give it a try and hire someone, and somebody else after that, until eventually five different people had been on my payroll. One of them had a great taste in music, and I kept him on longer than was reasonable because of the fine playlists he compiled for the office, and we are friends on Facebook still.

But I could not make any of them want to work. I always had the feeling they'd rather be in some other place, doing something else. Their heart was not in it, whereas mine is. I don't need to motivate myself, I love what I'm doing. I actually greet my stupid little office when unlocking it in the morning, and I love every minute I spend in here. My wife calls it the "Guillemin Museum" because of the way I decorated it to resemble an Art Deco bureau from the 1930s. It is exactly where I want to spend my working life.

But these people I hired were a different breed, and they puzzled me. It always seemed as if they were waiting for a curtain to rise and some kind of show to begin, with me as the puppet master. They expected me or any superior to be the string-pulling type. My first intern asked me why my phone does not ring more often. One started preparing meals in the kitchen, another liked to stay at the end of the day and hang around because of the good Wifi link. Not that I had failed to give them work to do. I just had no idea how to make them want to complete my assignments.

It was the classic leading-the-horse-to-the-water conundrum and quite hopeless. So, if they asked would it be okay to leave early, I said "By all means." If they wanted a day off, I told them "Knock yourself out." I'm no good at this, running the show, taking charge. I had assumed that leading by example would do the trick, but it did not. It could be that there is something wrong with my business model.

Many freelancers—or tradesmen of any sort, really—are introverts, living and working like hermits. They want to be left alone, concentrate on the job at hand, work the sun up and work it back down. They want the phone to hold its breath. Open-plan offices are the first circle of hell for them, cigarette breaks and after-hour drinking the stuff of nightmares, and staff Christmas parties worse than waterboarding. While I don't consider myself an introvert, I totally sympathise. If you enjoy being alone in your office all day and if you can make ends meet financially, look no further. You don't have to be an entrepreneur, and the notion of growth is not limited to quantity. You are at liberty to sell your services to whoever you fancy, and if that means you're selling yourself short, then that is your privilege. Small is beautiful, or can be, anyway.

Assuming you love what you're doing and that you hit the ground running in the morning, why would you want to bend over backwards to switch to a business model that lets you conquer and rule when you are neither the ruling nor the conquering type? Being an entrepreneur is not the only way to be content, nor is running a successful business the only measure of success, and the risks that come with either are formidable.

Nobody in their right mind would argue that the manager of a Nordic home furnishing store doing a roaring trade with flat pack furniture is happier than a cabinetmaker who completed a single table just the way the customer wanted it and who is now watching that customer circle the finished table in his shop, clucking happily.

Make Your Mark

My finest hour yet came one day when the personal assistant to a chief executive told him testily that "Mr Guillemin is the one who does this in Germany" while I waited on the phone, having explained to her that the job could not possibly get done by the time they needed it and that it was pointless to bring in other translators because they would not be familiar with the project even if I found any on short notice and because ultimately all of everything would have to be edited by me anyway.

Rather than repeating this lengthy spiel to her boss, who was in the same room, she simply elevated me to the status of the one authoritative English-German translator for real estate in Germany. "If only," my mind sighed while my heart skipped a beat. This happened years ago and I remember it still, not least because, sadly, it is no nearer to the truth now than it was then.

But for the sake of the argument, it nicely illustrates what it means to make your mark. Success in the corporate world hinges not so much on the quality of your product or service but on the way you present it. Your goodwill depends less on the unique selling proposition of your goods or services as such than on their foot print in the market. As long as you cleverly position it through search-engine optimisation, public relations and all the other razzle-dazzle of modern marketing, you don't actually need to manufacture your own product but might as well outsource its production. It is the well-known secret of Red Bull's success, a prospering company built on positioning itself as a lifestyle choice.

As a freelance translator, you have neither the resources to market your services in the conventional sense nor would you have the manpower to satisfy a sudden surge in demand if these marketing efforts paid off. And as mentioned in the introduction, I see no sense whatsoever in unsolicited advertising. Emails from freelance translators looking for work find their way into my in-box every day and I tend to delete them sight unseen. When I do take a look, they usually offer me a flurry of fields their senders cover in a number of languages at competitive rates and in no time at all. But how plausible is it that a single person has such a richly varied skill set yet values his services so little that he would sell them for a song?

To dispel doubt, these résumés often cite the names of satisfied prior clients, big names all of them from the corporate and institutional world, the United Nations and the European Union, NATO and NASA, Heaven and Hell. Yet here they are, out of work, sending pesky emails even to fellow freelancers like myself. I don't know for sure, but my guess would be that the only affirmative responses to these hapless pleas come from international translating sweatshops that pay little and late.

The thing is, it makes no sense for you to promise high quality translations because, frankly, you don't get to say. Your client does. If a service provider makes that kind of a claim, the opposite suddenly becomes imaginable: the idea that the service performance could fall short of the mark or has already done so in the past, necessitating a verification that you have done your homework since and are now up to par. Claims of this type are not just awkward, they backfire.

Someone contracting your services as a professional translator assumes that you know what you are doing. Of course, a first-time client not referred to you by one of your regulars may wish to know which other market players of relevance you work for, and in response to this inquiry you may flaunt your portfolio and name a few clients that mean something to that particular lead. The same is true for your expertise: A prospective client will only appreciate your know-how in one field, namely his or her own. The more areas you cover, the less likely it will seem that you are at home in the one area that matters to that client.

So, while it is a waste of time to advertise the high quality of your services, and while it makes even less sense to advertise it for a variety of areas and language pairs—after all, you are only one person—it does make sense to position yourself. As a lone warrior, you are better served by specialising in very few niches and very few languages. You simply cannot compete with agencies that cover everything, but you can make yourself an expert in your field and hone your reputation as a specialist. Naturally, you need not limit yourself to just one area and just one language pair as I do, but I am here to tell you that it works.

Your other forte as a freelancer, in addition to specialisation, should be flexibility. While you may have regular business hours, you should not feel bound to them, but be available on short notice, after hours, on holidays and weekends. You should offer turnaround times that agencies with no in-house translators can only dream of. You are not subject to any regulation protecting you from overtime or nightshifts, and you should make the most of it.

Your clients need not know how you get these stunts done. On the contrary, you should present a façade of effortless performance, giving your clients the feeling that you loved the challenge and that you are champing at the bit to do it again soon. Making them feel bad over your lack of sleep will get you nothing, least of all more rest, but may cause the relationship to sour. Not least, crazy work routines and night shifts come with their own motivational reward: There is a good chance that you will learn to love the quiet hours in the dark, with no one calling and the internet up to speed, because the monastic seclusion meets your introverted nature half way. Few things are as satisfying workwise as getting the kids ready for school *after* your first hand-off.

Over the years, the fine quality of your expert translations and the reliability of your deliveries will speak for themselves and take care of your positioning through networking. Of course, you will want to have your own homepage at your own top-level domain—a lean, clearly structured affair that profiles what you do, backed by a few client testimonials, not bold claims and glitzy images—and you will be a member of professional networks and associations that potentially could get you in touch with new clients (yet rarely do, which is why I won't even discuss them here).

In general, however, you will be passed around by returning clients and the client-side contacts you work with. Word will get around, and eventually personal assistants will whisper into executive ears that you cover exclusively their field, that you have done nothing else for years, that their direct competitors hire you, too, and that no agency comes even close. The key word is "years": You will be playing the long game, and there is no short-cut to building your reputation as a freelance translator.

However, the term "positioning" is not used here to gloss over the common wisdom that good workmanship advertises itself. Rather, the idea is to get to the point where your services help to position your clients. Much in the manner of fancy company cars, your services as a specialist translator will reflect favourably on the client buying them. Your good name will make your client look good, and don't be surprised if they insist on using your academic degree when addressing or recommending you. It makes them feel good about themselves—and thus about you. In other words, position yourself as an exclusive service provider, which is easy enough to do since there is only one of you. Make the limits of your one-man show work in your favour, true to the famous marketing ruse "It's not a bug, it's a feature."

An obvious way to enhance your exclusivity is your pricing. Charging rates close to the high end of the market will in itself signal confidence in your quality and reliability, both on your side and on the client side. Nice things cost money, goes the old adage, but psychologically the opposite is true as well: expensive things get more appreciation. Conversely, low-priced services tend to be seen as cheap, in every way. This need not cost you your competitive edge, because you can always offer a better bargain if you so choose. Use the same email you send to submit a quote at your standard rate to encourage your client to call you if he gets a lower quote from someone else and, if he does, negotiate a flat rate, for instance, or lower your rate in return for longer turnaround time. So that neither the client loses face nor you.

Generally, it has been my experience that clients care much more about reliable quality and prompt delivery than the costs thereof. Within reason, that is. Having your price ultimately works in the client's favour because you can spend more time on their assignments, and still have the revenues you need to cover your overhead.

Another way to attain exclusivity is by dropping accounts and turning down assignments. This option will not become relevant until your reputation as a specialist is firmly established and you are pressed for time, and even then, it can be dangerous. Being turned down might cause a returning client to feel unappreciated and you have to cite a plausible, pardonable reason for passing on a job. Do apologize, tell them to call again if the deadline is moved back, give them a good reason to return to you in the future, promise them a discount on their next assignment, because no one is too exclusive to be replaced. If you let an entire account go because it no longer suits your portfolio or field of expertise, make sure you burn no bridges. You may always fall on hard times and be grateful for every little job, no matter how remote from your standard line of work. But in general, making your services rare and hard to secure will elevate your status.

I personally am not comfortable enough yet to let fussy customers go just because I no longer have to worry about demand. However, there have been enough moments to vindicate the advice, for instance telling a mid-market manufacturer of electric motors that I'm really no expert in the field and telling someone in trade-fair organizing that I was simply overworked and had to divest myself of smaller accounts who only call once or twice a year. I made it more palatable and plausible by saying it was just for the time being. Of course, no level of specialisation will make me carefree enough to part ways with any of my real estate clients, even if I had reason to do so, and to start cherry-picking, but there is hope. Give me another twenty years and I may actually become exclusive enough to be considered "the one who does this in Germany".

Tell Tools from Toys

"The air is getting thinner!" a friend of mine gleefully told me some time ago, warning me that machines are about to make my trade obsolete. Who needs enemies when they have friends who call just to let you know that your goose is cooked? This friend was referring to a free online portal that will instantly translate any text you throw at it into a target language of your choice. The way this nifty robot plans to kill me is by pairing databases of existing translations with artificial intelligence. It is an engineering marvel and does an admirable job, but I don't think it will take my place or life any time soon.

Having checked out Mr Robot and having seriously wanted to like it, I found one of its major premises flawed. By definition, automated machine translation converts human text or speech from one natural language into another natural language without human intervention, following rules, statistics or neural networks instead.

This specific cyber translator returns properly structured sentences including subclauses, and it is easy to see how clients with limited language skills could be tempted to conclude that these are straightforward translations. The lack of stylistic finesse or awkward use of tropes is likely to bolster the impression.

However, there is a subtle fallacy at work here that may not reveal itself to the unsuspecting reader: One of the most basic underlying assumptions of machine translation is that the source text makes sense and will therefore lend itself to a meaningful translation. This is not necessarily the case, though, as other translators will confirm. Hastily composed source texts often contain grammatic, factual or logical errors on top of being stylistically sloppy, and this may not even be the result of poor penmanship but simply due to tight deadlines, for instance if the translating work for a bilingual brochure has to start before the source copy had been proofread so as to ensure both are ready to go to press at the same time.

The other day I realised that a text about Berlin submitted for translation must have been written by someone out of town, because it placed the radio tower on Alexanderplatz (which is the site of the TV tower, whereas the radio tower is at the fairgrounds) and the borough of Charlottenburg east of the borough of Mitte (the opposite being true). Minor factual errors such as these are easily detected or researched and corrected by a perceptive human mind.

In addition to delivering well-researched, fact-checked translations, translators can serve as something like a last-minute panic button, operating in the no-man's land between proofreading and publication and therefore having the unique opportunity to draw the client's attention to errors in the original text. It is an extra service they are not paid for but that—in my experience—is very much appreciated.

Another sentence I recently came across boasted that certain equipment "was upgraded to the latest standard" nine years ago. The sentence actually stated the year of the upgrade, and chances are that the text itself dated back to that time and had been recycled without checking its contents. A machine will translate this sentence faithfully, mindlessly—and thereby produce a translation that may actually harm your client with its absurd claim. Because in most industries, an upgrade nearly a decade ago hardly qualifies as the latest standard.

A third problem I often encounter are redundancies, like the one in the sentence "This building from the early twentieth century was raised in 1909." Which homebuyer would be unaware that 1909 is just a few years into the twentieth century? The human translator has the option to discuss it with the client and perhaps rephrase it. The machine does not. It may eventually become sophisticated enough to detect the logical issue, but will it be able to craft a better sentence and even if so, would we want it to?

For the time being, the dubious assumption that a given source text is accurate and actually signifies its intended signified renders automated machine translations as useless as Monty Python's "machine that goes ping." It is basically a fancy toy. Using it as a tool without human involvement would be reckless because the finished translation may contain no clues as to potential errors. And the risk that a given text contains subtle if decisive errors increases in proportion to its complexity.

I have seen automated translations of legal copy that communicated virtually the opposite of what the source passage said. You could lose your client or even be held legally accountable for this kind of mistranslation. Things get even trickier when it comes to the ambiguities and discursive layers of journalistic or fictional texts. And yet, this is not to disparage automated machine translation. Like many toys, it can be quite useful as long as you remember that it is just that, a toy and not a tool.

The proper tool of the professional translator—computer-assisted translation—also uses databases, except that these so-called translation memories (TM) are fed by you and/or by other human translators. Apart from your client base, the translation memories and glossaries you build up as freelance translator over the years constitute the closest thing to a goodwill. Your clients usually have no claims to your translation memories, for they paid only for the translations you prepared for them. If you were to sell your business, you could ensure the continuity of its performance and deliverables by selling your translation memories along with its client base. I, for one, am guarding my TMs like crown jewels.

Why am I saying this? At the time of this writing, the CAT software I'm using offers at least one add-on solution for automated machine translation that will integrate directly into your user interface. It will pre-populate the target segments and give you every opportunity to post-edit while learning from your editing and making adaptations. I know from a reliable source that it works amazingly well for their agency, and I have considered the proposition more than once. But I have not installed it, and my reluctance is motivated by more than just the risk of errors discussed above.

As a freelancer, you only have one brain to work with. In my case, that one brain, which has to do the translating, editing and proofreading, tends to get clouded by translations not mine. I have had the same problem when editing the translations of my employees: The prepopulated target segments obscured my idea of what I would have written unassisted. There is ample evidence in my translation memories that I let way too many mistakes or poor word choices slip in the past. Occasionally, I come across historic segments that were done by others but edited by me, and I'm appalled not so much by their poor quality as by my failure to recognise it at the time.

So, the very thought of having a machine pre-translate all of my text fills me with dread because I fear it would poison my entire database. Just to-day, in early 2019, Mr Robot offered me "unrest" for the German term "Unruhe" when the proper term would have been "unease." The German term can mean either, or indeed several other things as well, like "turmoil" or "turbulence," nuances that count. The context was Brexit, and if you ran a headline saying "unrest in the UK" people might start pouring into the streets of London spoiling for a fight. I'm dramatizing, but think of it: A sentence that looks innocent enough and properly phrased can be dead wrong, and how is the client supposed to be able to tell?

I'm all for efficiency, but not at the cost of my reputation. Once your professional standing as a third-party translator is compromised, there is no way to restore it. You might as well go into another line of business.

What I do instead of letting the machine do the work outright is that I use it to crosscheck my translations for useful alternatives. Whenever the need arises, I copy my source sentence into the mask of a machine translation portal to see what it comes up with. For some strange reason, I find it reassuring whenever its translations resemble my own—a deus-ex-machina phenomenon perhaps. Sometimes I'll borrow terms or sections from it, especially when I'm unhappy with my own work. But I won't install the app just yet. The other day, a German source text talked about a platform for estate agents, calling it a "Maklervermittler," a neologism for "broker of estate agents." But both "Makler" and "Vermittler" could arguably be translated with "broker" and so the MT portal offered me "broker broker" in an otherwise impeccably translated sentence.

It was there and then that I decided not to entrust the complexity of human discourse to the androids just yet. The automatic pre-translation feature of my CAT software is dangerous enough: In a list of place names, it recently translated the name of the German city of Essen with "Food" ("Essen" also being the word for either "meal" or "food") since it found that translation in the database.

I also resolved to include this caveat to know your toys from your tools in this chapbook. To be sure: I may be missing the boat, as my friend warned, but I'd rather see it leave without me than go down with it.

Tailor Your Text

Perhaps one of the hardest lessons to unlearn for the trained translator is to detach yourself from your source text. In my case, it took years to realise that my clients may—under certain circumstances—be better served if I do not faithfully translate the copy they submit to me. You certainly play with fire if you start putting yourself above the text you are supposed to transpose into another language. What I have in mind goes beyond standard methods a translator uses to keep the finished translation from sounding translated and therefore alien. Rather, the idea is to creatively rewrite the text in the target language to optimise it for its purpose and intended readership.

Taking this kind of liberty with your source text would be completely unacceptable for a court-appointed translator of legal copy. But it does have precedents in literary translations, most notably in the translation of children's books, where the objective is not to communicate certain information or to faithfully reiterate a tale even, but to make a story work and to ensure that someone reading the narrative in the target language is as willing to suspend his or her disbelief as a reader of the original is. Whenever a novel is re-translated, the new translation may be motivated not so much by the hope to deliver a more faithful translation but by the desire to make the novel more accessible for a contemporary audience—to make it a better read, as it were.

Most of the texts that come across my desk are penned by marketing or sales departments for the purpose of selling. Unlike legal notices, financial statements or general terms and conditions, whose translation is not open to interpretation, this type of text has a distinctly narrative quality to it and is more or less fictionalised. It talks less about the specifications of a given product than the imagined needs it will serve and the projected hopes it will fulfil. It speculates about desires and motives, makes assumptions about life styles, living standards and cultural backgrounds.

Getting on in years, I have become increasingly impatient with certain idiosyncrasies that, while harmless within their natural habitat, cause problems when taking out of it and transplanted into the alien environment of another language and culture. I'm sure that their authors are not even aware that the contents may be insensitive to the expectations of a foreign audience, nor do they ultimately have to be aware of it as long as their text inspires the intended response in the native crowd. In other words, my feeling is that I face a problem that my clients may not even know exists, and that they, if they did know, would advise me to address. It is this assumption that I cite to legitimise what I do to their texts.

Naturally, any language school and translating studies program will teach you not to mess with the source text. The standard setting in most CAT software actually makes it impossible to alter the wording of source segments. Which is as it should be, because even after many years in the business I would not dare doctor the source text. It isn't my text, it's the client's. My client-side contact has his or her own reasons to phrase things a certain way, and if poorly penned copy is the result of being overworked because three dozen sell sheets for different property developments are supposed to be online by the end of the week, so be it. It's none of my business. But the translation of the half-baked sell sheets is my business, and time has made me bolder to the point where I take liberties with the texts no teacher, state examination board or corporate editor would tolerate.

Reassuring to note, my clients like the subtle manipulation because they see in my translations the text they meant to write. As often as not, they are not even aware of any manipulation but think that this is a solid translation of what they wrote. The concept is not new at all, for these mimetic translations arguably follow the principle of localisation, most familiar from software translation: to adapt a software manual—including user interface terminology—to the cultural paradigm of the target audience, so that, pragmatically speaking, the instructions are equally intelligible in all of the languages they are translated into, and this precisely because culturally specific adaptations were made.

The sections below discuss several aspects that lend themselves to this sort of optimisation in translation. For obvious reasons, they will be illustrated with examples from my field of expertise—

German real estate—so that you will have to draw your own analogies to yours. I am positive the parallels will be easy to see. If you find the argument plausible and decide to try a similar approach, be subtle about it. There is always the risk that you misunderstand something so that modifying misunderstood contents could produce a blatant mistranslation. So, be careful, and do not consider this approach at all unless you are thoroughly familiar with your client's portfolio, corporate identity and clientèle as well as with the personality of your client-side contact.

FACTUAL: The details in the marketing text I get to translate are predictable and often narrow to the point of irrelevance for a foreign audience. Conversely, facts familiar to a native audience need to be elaborated for foreign readers and it can even make sense to add useful information not included in the German source text. For example, I tend to dilute the braggadocio used to parade "luxury bathrooms" when the supposed luxury it limited to high-end material and branded fixtures. At the time of this writing, truly posh interiors of the sort known to buyers from London or Paris are still the exception on the property market of the German capital. Similarly, while Berlin is largest city in Germany, it would be pointless to focus on its size for an international audience who associates the term "metropolis" with mega cities like Tokyo or Moscow.

Then again, you may want to expand a passing mention of towns in Brandenburg in your source text by adding that this is synonymous with the greater Berlin metro area because the State of Brandenburg surrounds the city on all sides. It is equally sensible, for instance, to distinguish precisely between Berlin's boroughs, districts and subdistricts even when the terms are used indiscriminately in the source text because locals can be expected to know the difference. Cover your back when doing so by following the terminology used by the relevant authorities or institutions, in this case the terms used by the Senate of Berlin on their own website. That way, you can be sure that the client's own web search will vindicate your word choice.

LOGICAL: If the causal chain that your source text follows fails to add up, research the facts and make the necessary adjustments to make the argument more plausible in your translation, meaning exactly in the way the author meant the text to work.

For example, a sell sheet I recently translated sought to make the condominium at hand more attractive by highlighting cultural amenities in the neighbourhood, and to this end described a nearby library as a place where "people can immerse themselves in books, papers and electronic media in various languages." It makes you wonder "as opposed to what?" and nicely highlights a rule I like to follow: It is pointless to make a statement whose opposite (in this case, a library not stocking these things) is unimaginable. Here, it would make more sense to quote the number of books in the library stacks or that the reading room has a great view, or other details you researched. This sort of modification will not at all compromise the purpose of the original argument but will back the claim with a more qualified argument in the target language. By contrast, you should not leave out the library altogether by talking about something else your research unearthed in the vicinity. Nor should you change the profile of the actual asset that is the subject of your text, because it is the client's right to present it any way he wants to, whereas the library has nothing to do with his business.

Mark me off as pedantic, but I also consider it a logical error if quantities or measurements are presented as approximations when they are arguably exact figures. Reading the line "the company has around 127 permanent staff" makes me want to pull my hair out, because that is a precise headcount of the workforce, not rounded at all. Neither is there anything rounded about an apartment sized "c. 180.7 sqm" because it simply does not get any more specific than that. The statement "the weighted average lease term is about 10.7 years" seems to suggest that you could quote this average figure down to the week or day, which no one would do. I'm not even going to elaborate why the promise that a given place is "located a walk of two-and-a-half minutes away" makes me cringe. Again, this may be nit-picking, but let me encourage you to hone your sensitivity for semantic incongruities you could iron out of your translation at no cost to its meaning.

STRUCTURAL: Imagine you are translating a letter by the board to its shareholders that starts by saying it's been a banner year, only to digress in the next sentence with a round-up of the ramifications that national and international politics have on the company's performance before reiterating that the past year has been good for business and why. Assuming you have translated similar letters for the same client in previous years and feel confident your meddling will be appreciated, you may wish to restructure the letter in your translation by starting with the global picture, then moving on to discuss the past, present and future of the company and ending with a passing mention of the outlook in global affairs.

I will sometimes go this far with clients I have served for a long time and who indulge me. Frankly, I would be at a loss what else to do with rambling key notes filled with anecdotal references to local or national events and idiomatic word plays that have no analogies in the target language. They would sound eccentric if you translated them verbatim, supposing they made sense at all.

I cannot speak for other languages, but at least in English, texts are expected to have a tripartite structure of introduction, argument and conclusion. In fact, every paragraph should be structured as a self-contained unit. As my clients are unaware of or indifferent to this principle, I feel it is my responsibility to consider it in their stead. I'm sure if I explained to them that English texts tend to have a more rigid structure, they would come out and ask me expressly to adjust my translations accordingly for maximum effect. Since few people have time to engage in theoretical discussions of this sort, I simply go ahead and reorganise sentences in subtle ways, waiting for someone to cry uncle. No one ever has.

Another option for structural modification that is subtler and much more effective concerns the sentence structure. At first glance, your client may not even notice the difference to the source text after you resorted to this option. My own clients have occasionally commented that a given translation sounds almost better than the original, and attributed it to the elegance of the English language.

German prose can be every bit as elegant, but German copy writers have traditionally favoured nouns and nominalisations because they sound more authoritative and factual in the manner of rules and regulations. English, by contrast, puts a premium on verbs and verbal phrasing although it is as easy to nominalise verbs in this language as it is in German. Two grammatical peculiarities support this, one being the position of the entire verb clause in the front section of an English sentence, the other being the common use of the present participle, whose German equivalent is rarely used. Since it is phonetically identical to the gerund—one of the options to nominalise a verb—the present participle neatly combines the syntactic function of the verb with the semantic authority of the noun.

The sentence "The plans of the company provide for further property acquisitions and sales with a view to the optimisation of its portfolio" becomes more legible when replacing some of the nouns with verbs so that the rephrased sentence reads "the company plans to keep buying and selling property with a view to optimising its portfolio." The first version is structured like a typical

German sentence, the second like an English one. The example is made up and exaggerated, but you can usually tell that a close translation from German by its over-reliance on nouns and nominalised verbs.

The observation is, of course, not my own, and you may actually remember it from linguistics class. But if you are new to the actual business, fresh out of school, you may not be aware that some of the style guides issued to translating agencies by global software vendors mandate that you prioritise the use of verbs and verbal phrasing to make their manuals more legible. I remember, for instance, the instruction to use nominalised verbs in serialised headlines of German translations just to minimise the use of nouns.

Since you are probably a trained linguist anyway, and since the situation may be slightly different for your language pair, there is no point in expanding on the methodological side of it. But principally, it is safe to say that most translations communicate their contents more effectively if you convert some of the noun phrases into verb phrases.

That being said, rewriting a client's text in another language means to lean very far out of the window. When in doubt, you should definitely discuss the idea with your client, providing examples of what you have in mind. After all, it could end up as a well-intended effort that goes horribly wrong. No one who worked for me ever submitted alternatives I was willing to accept after I had encouraged them to rephrase or restructure.

Even when it comes to something as innocent as Christmas cards—whose English phrasing several clients leave entirely up to me—it is of the essence to strike just the right note, or you'll make matters worse than a direct translation, which always has that excuse of being obviously a translation. But if you get it right in a way your client appreciates, it is an opportunity to shine that puts instant machine translation in its place.

CULTURALLY: By translating a text, you arguably prepare it for export, even if its recipients live or work in the same country. Most of the texts I get were written for the domestic audience, the decision to have them translated often made later and without any thought to their effectiveness outside their native cultural realm. Again, I feel that the translator has a unique opportunity and responsibility to identify and possibly address sensitive issues that may not be relevant in the domestic context. Some years ago, I saw a ham-fisted poster advertising German pork by showing a skimpily dressed blonde girl cooking or eating it. Thank goodness I did not have to translate it, but it made me wonder: What sort of response will it provoke in a Muslim, in an African or even in white middle-class Americans with their skewed view of Germany as the land of well-endowed frauleins and big sausages?

Few of the stereotypes I find in source texts are this blatant, but as a translator, you are naturally more likely to be aware of them than others. The same goes for culturally motivated differences in priorities and interests. An overseas investor trying to commit his money in a stable market like Germany will care less about infrastructure and greenery in the area than a domestic home buyer. Foreign companies entering the German market are probably more interested in high-speed connectivity than the richly varied night life. If they hail from the Middle East, they may find it irritating if one property sales kit after another includes references to places where alcohol is consumed and the sexes mingle.

Something that has been truly getting on my nerves is the apparently compulsive mention of good ways to relax. I have yet to see a marketing text for German real estate of any type (with the possible exception of logistics warehouses) that does not promise places for relaxation on or off the premises. The other day, a web profile praised a condominium for its "ample space to relax, recover and take it easy." Is that all anyone does do at home? How do you differentiate between the three? And what does the prospective buyer do for a living that drives him to such exhaustion? What bothers me, of course, is the cliché of the strict distinction between professional and private life in a time when more and more people work from home, be it part time or full time. How about advertising a loft whose floor plan accommodates a family of five plus a workplace? How about selling the penthouse to someone who does not care about a hedonistic lifestyle and never entertains but wants to practice martial arts up there? Hedonism is not an imperative but a lifestyle choice. But forgive me: I seem to have gone off on a tangent here.

Other clichés that should be reviewed and tempered by the translator include superlative claims at the expense of other nations, because the reader will by definition be an outsider or else will have other reasons to doubt that a given entity, place, product or service is superior to their equivalents in his or her home country. One characteristic many of the German texts share is their focus on the first person singular or plural: Here is what we already did, here is what we do now, and here are the wonderful things available from us. It is an attitude motivated by a performance-centred marketing approach typical of German companies. The logic behind it is to win your confidence and business by presenting a good scorecard.

The marketing paradigm of Anglo-Saxon players differs in a subtle but decisive shift from the first to second person: Let us show you what we can do—for you! Call it calculated modesty or plain good manners, English marketing speak puts the reader at the centre.

At least that has been my impression, another one being that foreign readers can be irritated by the Germans talking mainly about themselves. Especially Americans see what Germans consider straightforward honesty as brash and uncivil whereas Germans, in turn, often find the formal civility of Americans "phoney." As a translator, I arguably play an ambassador between the realms of my language pair, and so I have made it my business to shift the focus away from the "me" to the "you" in my translations into English when it is safe to do so and in ways subtle enough to be acceptable to my clients.

STYLISTICALLY: As a trained language specialist, you need no advice on how to enhance your translations stylistically. Your fluent use of styles and registers—and conversely your frustration with the humdrum routine of pre-scripted agency work—probably made you bold enough to go it alone in the first place.

But there is one thing you may not have considered: Your personal stylistic standard may not be the best style for your client's translations. Imagine your name was Winston Churchill and you got the job to translate all the marketing material of the foreign carmakers for the United Kingdom. Suddenly, the brochures of the French car manufacturers would sound just like those of their Japanese competitors, and all of them would sound like Prime Minister's Questions in the House of Commons.

Since you will normally—having specialised in a field—serve a number of clients in the same industry, you should ensure that each speaks with a distinct voice in your translations. If your client already has a homepage in the target language, look no further and adopt its style. If your translations are the client's first in that language, let the homepages of his competitors in the target market inspire you. If you have a by-line article to translate for a trade paper, check the rhetoric commonly used in that publication and emulate it. Striking the right note from the start could actually make the paper's editor your ally when your client finds fault with your product. In a case like this, the extra time spent researching styles will be well worth it if it saves you revisions and discussions.

Another piece of advice I'd like to share because I learned it the hard way is to keep your translations simple and easy to understand. "There is no need to be fancy," someone told me when we jointly worked on a translation, and right he was. There is a German saying that it's not the angler who is supposed to like the bait, but the fish. Yet experience shows that my clients want to understand and like my translations, and that they hate it if the translations makes them feel stupid because it uses three-syllable words or idioms.

There is reason to the madness: My English translations are meant to address anyone whose first language is not German. They are supposed to be simple. So rather than penning lines you could deliver with relish at the Oxford Union, I'm expected to speak an English that investors from Milan, Madrid and Marseille will understand without a dictionary. A Euro-English no native of the British Isles would want to be associated with, but which is optimised for its purpose.

Give your clients what they want. Since they are the ones footing your bill, you should provide the kind of rhetoric they prefer, not least because they may have to use it in meetings and presentations. You don't want to embarrass them.

Here as elsewhere, keeping your eyes open is of the essence in order to detect and defuse sensitive issues and to make your translation every bit as effective for a foreign readership as the source text is for the domestic one. It is one of the main ways in which the freelance translator can outperform agencies, which lack the time for such finesse, and machine translation solutions, which are not yet ready to cope with this degree of complexity. If you are good at dressing your clients' language, and if your clients know that your work makes them look good, they will choose your tailored translations over off-the-shelf product any day.

Play the Nerd

The majority of emails sent to me seem to reflect a tacit understanding that proper phrasing, spelling and interpunction are a nice-to-have luxury that those who are pressed for time can ill afford. And everyone is pressed for time all of the time. Any professional worth his or her salt conducts their business at break-neck speed to overachieve and outperform, and a sloppily drafted email carries a sense of contained urgency reflecting the fact. By reverse argument, a spell-checked, proofread email would seem to suggest that you are not quite serious about your business because you appear to have extra time on your hands, time to waste on pedantic frills like commas and hyphenation.

However, in a professional who works with language, it literally indicates lack of composure and thus arguably a lack of business acumen. It suggests a frantic rather than a brisk performance. After all, grammar and orthography were not invented by some über-schoolmarm to torment you but are the product of a perennial effort to make language more efficient. When wielded by the professional, language becomes a precision-engineering tool that can do anything and that is most precise in legal copy: omit or add a single period from your translation of a legal document and you may be in deep trouble.

To me personally, the sophisticated rhetoric that multinational corporations or foundations use in their fancy ads sound like music despite their terseness and whimsical propositions. It contrasts starkly with the marketing texts that the authors of the careless emails dump into my lap for me to translate. As often as not, these texts are as erratically composed as the electronic notes that announce them. Which brings me to my point:

There is no way to communicate more swiftly than in a properly phrased sentence. And to the trained mind, phrasing such a sentence requires little or no extra effort. And even if it did, you should pretend that it does not, because you claim to be a language professional. Aside from efficient communication, the correspondence with your clients presents one of the few opportunities for you to show how adept you are not in your target language (presumably your native tongue) but in your clients' own language. If your clients can see for themselves how varied your vocabulary is and how meticulous your interpunction, they have reason to assume that you will be using the same kind of diligence when working on their assignments. So, especially if you translate into a language a given client does not speak, you should seize the chance to impress. Finish your sentences, get the apostrophes right, dot your i's and cross your t's, in a manner of speaking. Be the diligent nerd. It does not mean you have to be dull.

For the same reason, give yourself a no-nonsense façade that will tell leads and clients that you are as serious about your business as an established translating agency. Demonstrate that you are neither a student doing this temporarily, nor a bohemian doing it on the side to pay for rent and groceries. There are few ways to present yourself to advantage physically because your interaction with your clients will almost exclusively be conducted through telecommunication of one sort or another. This makes it all the more important to have a proper homepage with your own domain. That way, your correspondence will be channelled not through a free network account but carry your domain name in every email. Have your homepage properly designed by someone you pay and have it optimised for search engines so that entering "translations" and the name of your home town and your field of expertise will bring your name up on the first page.

Have neat stationary on expensive paper printed in a print shop, carrying your name and possibly your logo in a way that could not be produced by an office printer, and use it for your postal correspondence, most notably your invoices. Model your letters and invoices on specimen you find on the internet, again to simulate a regular agency. Have handsome business cards designed and printed for the occasional meeting. Put a proper plaque on the front door of your office and fit out one room as a presentable meeting room, unless you work from home or rent coworking space, in which case it is a better to invest in your personal outfit and go see the client whenever the need for personal face-time arises.

All of these things (except the personal outfit) are tax-deductible business expenses, so there is no need to be squeamish. One of my personal frolics is to design bi-lingual Christmas cards with a freely phrased message that goes out in customised envelopes to anyone who has done business with me that year. It is one of the few opportunities for me to showcase creativity in both source and target language and a spare-no-expense attitude toward my business. You may not wish to go that far, but the long and the short of it is: Cultivating a conventional business front should be a calculated effort that helps you to position yourself as a level-headed partner.

Groom Your Avatar

My life, especially my working life, would be so much easier if I sounded like the late great James Coburn, or so I believe. As a third-party provider working remotely for whoever I happen to be working for, I spend a fair share of my time on the phone, discussing the exciting things my client and I are planning to do, and spending the rest of my time imagining how awesome it would have been to carry my end of the conversation in the deep grovelling voice of James Coburn, sounding mildly belligerent yet somehow warm, like everyone's avuncular friend and the man who gets things done. People would order more, pay more for what they ordered and never question my delivery dates or word choices if I was channelling James Coburn on the phone.

Or would they, really? Of course, I'm not even going to dignify that with an answer, because the question is missing the point every bit as much as the teenage girl who wonders should she have cosmetic surgery done. However, the predicament prompting either question is very real, and there is a name for it: insecurity. While the reason for the teenager's insecurity are as obvious as her prospects of getting over it, the case of the insecure freelance translator is more complex. This is not to suggest that every freelancer is insecure, but many people who spend vast amounts of time by themselves tend to become introverts, or vice versa. Which in turn makes them prone to be less sure of themselves when out in public than gregarious people are. To me personally, feeling unsure of yourself seems a perfectly plausible response to a world where few things are certain, and so I won't attempt to question the fact or the causes of someone's insecurity.

The only question I will address here is whether there are any easy ways to cope with it in a manner that is reassuring for the client. Being alone at your desk or at home, you can be anything you like, a manic depressive or Bozo the Clown, but you may want to keep a lid on it because it is nobody else's business, least of all your client's. On the contrary, it is of the essence to present an intact front to the client. You should never, ever position your working self as something other than a beacon of integrity. In the same sense that a company is more than the collective personality of its workforce, you should pass yourself off not as a person, but as a one-person brand. I like to think of this face you present to your client base as an avatar, like in a video game—composite yet not unreal, superhuman yet a recognisable individual.

Let me illustrate the avatar concept with a story. When we were children, my little sister used to be shy to the point of muteness in the presence of grown-ups, except in one situation: in my uncle's car on the motorway at night. My uncle drove fast, at least compared to our dad's glacial pace, and we loved getting to ride in his car, but none more so than my little sister. In Winnie-the-Pooh's world, she would have been Piglet, but night rides on the motorway turned her into Tigger. When he took us back home from our cousins' in the evening, she would pipe up in the backseat where the grown-ups in front could not see her, and comment on everything on or off the road vociferously, brashly, glibly, only to fall silent once the dome light came on in the driveway. My uncle turning in his seat to compliment her on the sassy run-on commentary would only find us boys in the back seat and a wan voiceless little waif, frozen in the headlights of adult discourse.

I have taught myself to match her act on the phone and in email correspondence. Over the years, I learnt that personal encounters with my clients should be avoided. Such meetings tend to be on the executive level, e.g. with heads of departments or authorised signatories in attendance, because the only reason for a freelance translator to meet a client-side representative in person is to negotiate and sign a contract. Everything else is easier and more efficiently done over the phone and via email or snail-mail correspondence.

I shudder when thinking back to some of these meetings in my early years: There I would be, in my one good jacket, standing less than six foot tall, cowed by the glitzy corner office of an alpha male, fumbling my words, presenting an awkward business case, consenting to ridiculous conditions and still leaving with the distinct sensation that my interlocutors were the ones who felt let down. Even the secretary seemed to watch me exit after such a lacklustre performance with a mildly scandalised frown, as if she would now charge me for the coffee she had enthusiastically served—compliments of the house—upon my arrival.

On the phone or in writing, however, this stick-figure me turns into "the urban professional" who, in addition to being at the top of his game, has a well-rounded personality and many interests, family and friends, sports and hobbies, a flurry of likeable vices and, naturally, a fine sense of humour. This is the back-seat act you want to hone: Hint at resources and capacities that will make up for the lack of manpower in a jiffy even if it's really you and your tools, working double shifts. Admit that you love being a super-lark who gets up at the crack of dawn. Confess to your creative side, that you love writing even when not writing for your clients.

While many of these traits are not necessarily contrived, it might in the eyes of some people seem phoney or downright dishonest to instrumentalise them. But if you stop short of bragging, this subtle display of confidence gives your clients the sort of reassurance they need before they entrust their business to you. Of course, you should not make things up or inflate them. Just juggle them a bit for effect, present yourself to advantage, by no means to deceive the client but precisely to defuse a latent, if persistent, fear on the client side that a freelancer is self-employed only because he found no other employment and that he might fail them in the same way he must, no doubt, have failed previous employers.

In the eyes of the permanently employed, it is a thin line that separates the lone-wolf entrepreneur from the ne'er-do-well misfit, and you should put everything you have into a glossy façade of professional conduct to refute that suspicion. What do you know about your client's integrity? There is a good chance that the over-achiever has bungled several marriages and cries himself to sleep at night in front of the TV. But in the daytime, he will waltz with you if—and only if—you know your well-rehearsed steps and know your place.

If you feel this sounds a lot like old-school discipline, let me tell you that playing by rules has worked a treat for me as long as I am the one making those rules. One of the most effective regiments is to pretend that you keep regular business hours on weekdays. During my own business hours, I habitually answer the phone on the second ring and reply to emails within minutes. For the same reason, I watch the phone ring off the hook on weekends, not touching it even if I'm in the office, lest my clients think I'm a workaholic with no social life. Never tell a client that you worked the entire weekend to get an assignment done, but just say it was a challenge you were happy to meet. What good would it do you long-term if you made the client feel bad about having ruined your weekend? None at all. He or she would hold it against you and think you are poorly organised.

Here is another one of my silly little rules: Always let your clients know how good it is to hear from them, and that you will see what you can do even if you are completely booked out. There is always a way to rearrange your schedule, granting discounts for extended deadlines and charging extra for rush jobs. And even if you have to pull out of a job later on, doing so will be more convincing after you displayed initial optimism.

What I am about to say is not meant flippant or exploitative in any kind of way, but is my unambiguous advice: Call them by name on the phone, remember the names of their children and the holidays they told you about, say something nice about the town they are calling from, take an interest, show that you care. If someone returns from maternity leave, ask her how the baby is doing and she herself. After a period of having actively cultivated this phone etiquette, it will become self-sustaining, because you will realise you enjoy interacting with live beings and that you take pleasure in the small talk, the human touch. You really will care.

Inversely, the people at the other end will remember you fondly and take you with them when they move on, which is something I carefully strive for as my most effective networking approach. After about a minute of socialising, ask them in midsentence in a briskly friendly business voice what you can do for them today.

A final example: Never share concerns over finances or taxes, and never cast doubt on your performance or outlook. Like they say in the movies, anything you say can and will be used against you—even and especially your worries. Your clients owe you nothing but cold cash, and they will feel so much better about giving it to you if you do not make them uncomfortable but make them feel good about working with you, that is, if you present an avatar they understand and like. And hey: It does not have to be James Coburn.

Dodge the Bullies

Originally, this chapter was supposed to be head-lined "Beware of Psychopaths," but there is no need to dramatize things. They are dramatic enough as it is. Someone who worked for a certain client of mine called him, his boss, a psychopath during a conversation with me, laughing it off as if he was stating the obvious. To me as an outsider, it was far from obvious and it came as a small shock.

At the time of that conversation, I had groomed his boss, my client, for nearly a decade and believed my standing with him and within his company was unassailable. Having learned to handle the unpredictable mood swings and whims of a choleric father, I took pride in being good at this game. In another life or another era, I would have excelled as an aide-de-champs to an irascible commander, or so I thought. I never contradicted this client, had accepted nearly unacceptable terms to get his account, had done favours for free and always been on hand, worked nights and weekends, had never forgotten my place. My strategy had been to make myself an asset, the same strategy that his personal assistant seemed to be following, and the objective was to be eventually rewarded not just with a secure client account, nor even with better terms but with a co-dependence that went beyond the business relationship.

You can probably tell things did not work out along these lines. Looking back, I wonder what made me so optimistic. But I am still amazed by the speed with which things fell apart, for I lost this account of nine years in the blink of an eye, and over nothing at all.

Some weeks earlier, I had finally flipped and snapped back at him over the phone when he had gone on another rant. We made up, parted on amicable terms, but a short while later one of his assistants, a newbie in the PR department, let me know that my services would no longer be required. My work was not up to the standard they were used to. After nearly a decade. When I called the client himself to make sure this was not done without his knowledge, he confirmed that he was aware of the dismissal and that there was nothing he could do. "I never involve myself in these decisions," he wrote in his email, although he was the one who had dictated his business terms and prices to me. Of course, the whole affair was much more complex, with other factors and incidents playing a role. But what I came to learn is that nothing you do or refrain from doing will secure you the lasting loyalty of a narcissistic alpha male.

I see no point in learning this through first-hand experience. You can save yourself a lot of trouble if you watch for certain tell-tale signs and to pull up your stakes before the exploitative relationship with a narcissist can seriously hurt you. What makes this easier is their stinginess with money and praise. They can simulate gratitude until they are in control but they are not grateful. If you excel, the credit for your performance goes to them for having given you the opportunity. They would prefer not to have to pay you at all because you are already blessed with the privilege of getting to do business with them, but they understand that it is standard practice to do so.

In the case above, my client got me to translate a biweekly newsletter of around five pages for free in return for recommending my services to his clients. He thought this a fair deal and assumed that I was acquiring a steady stream of new clients that way. He was not being cynical, he truly believed this, and he would have been appalled to realise that what really made it worth my while was his high staff churn. People used to come and go at his firm as if they were visiting the circus. Few people are prepared to be bullied anymore and many will rather lose a job than subordinate themselves. What worked in my favour was the productive cooperation between them and myself during their brief stints and the fact that many of them would remember me whenever they needed a translator at their next place of employment. Some of the relations established at the time survive to this day.

Of course, there is always a bright side to things, but this latter benefit—which I call the "dandelion effect" because the quick dispersion of young talent resembles that flower's downy seeds carried on the breeze—hardly made up for my colossal error in judgement. Apart from the financial trouble the unexpected loss of this account caused me, I felt humiliated, not least when I discovered a testimonial by this entrepreneur on the homepage of the agency that replaced me, which stated not just how satisfied he was to have found such "a reliable and competent partner" but also that he had never considered anyone else in the past ten years, i.e. during the years I had worked for him at a discount any time he needed me. My initial reaction was to feel betrayed.

When another narcissist, his business not quite as important to me, dropped me as a provider with the vague explanation that he wanted to "try someone else" I had the distinct feeling he wanted to hurt me. There had been an explicit understanding that I would only take the trouble of extracting the texts of his homepage into a file for the sake of compiling a quote and then translating them if the job was mine for the asking and the submission of a quote but a formality. Feeling let down, I was tempted to think that this type of person will stab you just to watch you bleed. Simply because they have the ability and opportunity.

And I felt like the victim of a power game when a publisher whom I thought to have befriended cut me off from further assignments, arguing I had virtually ruined a certain book project by failing to

work with his in-house team and missing deadlines. I thought he was kidding because he himself
had assigned a contact to me whom I had met and
collaborated with. The book had been published as
planned and continues to be available. I was
stunned to find that he was serious. It seemed almost sadistic at the time.

Looking back, however, I must say that there
was no malice involved in any of these cases. Just
a personality disorder, an almost pathological lack
of sensitivity and empathy. The narcissist entrepreneur wants to be at the centre of things, and not
just the big things. He wants to dominate the line
of business he is in, his social environment and
most of all his biography. His compulsive preoccu-
pation with himself makes his performance,
achievements, aspirations the subject of every conversation, and he will listen only long enough to
find the cue for his next monologue.

One offered me office space to set up a bigger
operation, and it seemed like a generous offer until
he quoted the net income he expected to get out of
it by the end of the first year, a sum so wildly out of
touch with the reality of the translation business

that I realised it was just another attempt to take charge of something not yet his.

The rash decisions and erratic shifts in attitude are solely motivated by an obsession to occupy centre stage. It does not even matter what stage it is and which play is being performed, as long as they play the lead. In fact, none of the narcissist clients I've dealt with bore me any ill will. On the contrary, despite their business prowess they had the emotional intelligence of infants, helplessly addicted to praise and fawning for attention while completely unaware of their constant transgression of boundaries. They were nonplussed by the carousel of employees coming and going, thought them lazy or stupid, spoiled brats of one sort or another, felt misunderstood when confronted with their own aggressive behaviour and demands. They had elaborate theories how to become a self-made man, but they had neither families nor spouses and no idea why.

So, my advice to you is simple: Stay away from narcissists or ogres, as my wife calls them. There is no failsafe way to ensure their loyalty, no golden rule to go by. What made them happy yesterday will make them go berserk tomorrow and vice versa, and showing unwavering dedication as an outsider is a sure way to get ditched. One of the ogres I mentioned above brought an entire case of vodka to his company's Christmas party one year just to watch his employees make fools out of themselves. Himself a teetotaller and athlete, he watched them the way Circe must have watched Ulysses' men with a mixture of fascination and disgust as they turned into swine, being sick all over the place. A gentle person, astute and soft-spoken, lethal as a snake but without malice.

How can you tell you are dealing with a narcissist? Don't worry, you will know. After all, being allergic to being told what to do is probably part of the reason why you became self-employed in the first place. If not, just trust your senses: If something seems wrong, it is wrong. If a new client yells at you, makes inroads on your private life, blames you for problems he has no interest in solving, then just put down the phone gently and cluck your tongue. Tell them you are booked out or whatever. One time I backed out of a contract citing health reasons. The ogre's secretary called, not knowing what to make of it. But health is nothing you can negotiate, and she knew it.

A final piece of advice: Don't ever lose your composure when bullied. Neither contradict nor explain. Any defence or counterargument will be taken as a vindication of the criticism. You cannot win, because there is nothing to gain. More important yet, you never know when you may need them again. Ogres are powerful, well-networked and surprisingly forgiving. The ones I told you about are always happy to see me or talk to me, either unaware of past differences or pretending to be. They like me for letting them kill me and for being docile about it. Next time you run into one at a conference or trade fair, make sure you compliment him on whatever he happens to be doing and he will treat you to a childlike smile.

Take Care of Yourself

Working alone has its perks, no doubt about it. Getting to keep your own hours, to have your own space that lets you focus on your work without the bustle of an open-plan office, to take breaks when you need them rather than at stated times, to have to answer to no co-worker, superior or subordinate—all of this is wonderful and its wonder won't wear off.

Yet in many ways, the freelance translator is out on a wire without a net. Safeguards familiar from agency work are not in place, such as project manager, language lead, proof-reader or the checks and balances of team work in general. Missing a step might cause you to fall—to stay with the image—and no one will catch you, nothing cushion your fall. Handing in bad work could cost you an account. Losing a multiplier, meaning a consulting agency through which you serve several clients, could even cost you your livelihood.

On a less dramatic note, having to personally take care of the unproductive parts of your business, such as the administrative end, the research and the preparation of files for translation, will sap your efficiency. A substantial share of your workday will not be billable hours but will be spent with phone calls and correspondence, quotes and research, computer updates and taxes. Especially if business is good, you will have no time to be ill or to go on holiday. Whenever business is slow, there is no way to tell when it will gather momentum again, if ever.

If you see no need for so much doom and gloom, chances are that you are just starting out as a freelancer. It probably means that you are healthy, young and single and that you have not considered what the potential implications of self-employment are when you get older, have a family to feed and your health begins to fail. This chapter may be the most boring yet because it will sound like the parental piece of advice you chose to ignore. I would not blame you if you prefer not to read it at all, because I could not have cared less at the time I started out in the early zero years.

But I'm including it anyway so that, if you prefer to take a rain check now, you can read it later as some sort of consolation when things get tough.

Perhaps you will then take comfort in the knowledge that you are not alone and that others have survived the same kind of trouble. That things will pass. All of the advice provided in the following section are meant to stave off or contain the hazards of self-employment and have a common theme: creating safeguards.

Let us start with the most obvious safeguard because it's all in the name: Get insurance, meaning the types of insurance that make sense for you, and get it as early as you can. You may not be legally required to pay into social security or a pension scheme. And even though health insurance is mandatory (at least in Germany), there are ways to drop out.

When I started out as freelancer, I decided I could not afford the expense and bought no health insurance, until I realised after a few short years that the opposite was true: I could not afford to go without. Even if you are young and healthy, you do need dental care. So, I was lucky that the health insurance of my student years took me back when I needed major dental work. It is in any case a gamble, since you are always just one accident away from a fat hospital bill.

What makes it sensible to start paying into a pension plan early on is the swift passage of years. Let's assume you graduate in your mid to late twenties and decide to go without for a few years until you make good money and can afford it: If you start paying into a scheme ten years later, you will have less than 30 years until your retirement age, and your payments will be so high that they will feel at least as inconvenient as the smaller payments would have felt a decade earlier.

There is also a good chance that your expenses will have gone up in sync with your income. There never will be a time when money is just laying around the house. So, unless you are waiting to come into an inheritance, do take out a life insurance or a government-sponsored pension plan regardless of how boring that seems. Speaking of which, life insurances are a bag full of tricks, because you can borrow against them, use them as collateral or even sell them. At maturity, you can choose to have them paid out in a lump sum with a premium that puts certain other risk-free investments to shame or choose to draw monthly payments for the rest of your life.

On a cautionary note, let me add that getting disability insurance makes no sense at all for a translator, first of all because the rates are staggering, and secondly because, with translating being the equivalent of an easy office job, I don't know what would have to hit you to convince the insurance company that you are disabled. You would have to be blind and brain-dead to become eligible, at which point you would be past caring anyway.

I personally see no sense in legal insurance (to cover legal fees) either because it is always better to avoid a legal dispute by backing down and settling out of court. The high-octane lawyers your client can sic on you will always be feistier and smarter than whoever your insurance company has on retainer for a freelance translator. Of course, that is just my opinion, but so far, I've been able to sort out every dispute before it got serious—by being conciliatory and cooperative.

Another piece of advice is to take a holistic approach, especially if you are in a relationship or have a family. Since your income as a freelancer tends to follow cycles, with ups and downs, it would be ideal if your partner held down a regular job with a steady income. Apart from the pay check, this would have the added benefits of covering your partner's health insurance and social security, plus he or she would get paid vacations, paid sick leave and a Christmas bonus (again, this may just be the case in Germany), and if you have children, their health insurance is usually covered too. These perks make a huge difference, because private health insurance and life insurance for each child add up quickly.

For a few years, my wife worked in my office as well, the idea being to keep the money in the family and to double the punch of the family business. But somehow things just failed to work out, because it was awkward for me to be her superior, to advise and instruct her, and to correct her work. She never got into it. Things may be different for you, especially if you both started out as translators, but having my wife accept a permanent job turned out a much better arrangement for us, not least because of the option to take the day off if one of the children falls ill. Before that, the ailing child would camp out in my office for the day.

Thirdly, you need to develop routines to maintain your health. If you work half the day at the desk, staring at a screen, you should make sure you get out in between, before or after your work. Exercising regularly outdoors will not only balance your sedentary work life but also help you clear your head and work out issues on the job, to say nothing of other issues like stress or frustration. I keep my running gear right in the office, and during the wintertime when the sun sets in the late afternoon, I head out for a spin in the nearest park in mid-day. If you miss a call that way, your client will automatically assume you are out to lunch, literally speaking. In the summertime, running early in the morning when it's still cool is an excellent way to get ready for a day cooped up in the office.

If you work long hours and get little night time sleep, try taking brief power naps in the daytime. I have a couch in the office, mainly for that purpose. Some days, I take three or four ten-minute naps whenever fatigue sets in and still lose less than an hour overall. Both the exercise and the naps cut up an otherwise long day into efficient stints, and they are paced by the body's needs, not a set schedule. Of course, you should do this only during busy times, like ahead of trade fairs, and eventually return to getting a good night's sleep. Since your body supports your brain, and since the one sine-qua-non asset of your business is your mind, you must do everything you can to keep your body in shape.

For the same reason, you need to give your mind regular breaks from translating. Get it interested in something different, a hobby or craft or even charity work, the latter having the added benefit of putting your own woes in perspective. It should be active and creative, and your heart should be in it, and it should not just be a pastime. Least of all, it should be watching TV or gaming because you need to spend time away from screens if you work a full day in front of the computer. Reading books is an obvious choice because of your affinity to language, but again, it makes sense to let your eyes rest.

Doing things with your hands can be particularly rewarding because of the tangible result you produce—quite the exotic experience for a service provider who tends to get feedback only after botching a job. What do I do? Taking pictures, losing at chess against my sons, giving rusty old objets trouvés a new purpose, e.g. turning a segment of Belle Époque balcony railing into a wall-mounted coat rack, and—wait for it—writing silly books.

Last, but not least, you should create emotional safeguards, meaning outlets and sources of sustenance. If you have family or a partner, share your frustrations and issues with them, even when you don't expect any solutions from them. Especially children will put things in perspective, but hanging out with friends or colleagues in the sense of a third place can have the same effect. In my experience, the very act of putting pent-up concerns into words that others understand will often relativize them.

The solitary work style of the freelance translator needs a regular reality check lest you start fretting over imaginary problems. One good way to dispel concerns is, of course, to discuss them with the respective client right away. Chances are that a given problem seemed larger than it actually is, that a deadline can be moved or that an invoice was lost in the mail and will be paid as soon as you re-submit it. Some of the trade associations for the translating and interpreting sector organise seminars and local roundtables for shop talk or just for getting together while some CAT software vendors host webinars and blogs. Check around, socialise with other freelancers and quit being a recluse at quitting time. Doing so is also a good way to stay up to date on latest trends and rules, products and upgrades, jobs and projects, events and people.

When push comes to shove, it can get quite lonely for the freelancer, to the point of despair. I, for one, have occasionally felt a distinct urge to surrender, but since I'm not fighting a war, there is no enemy to surrender to. Yet the desire to have the option to wave a white flag will visit you from time to time, when you cannot sleep at night over the relentlessness of it all. The worries rarely ever stop, and you can never lean back, because everything depends on you and your health. It may get easier over time, but I will never be easy. Do not believe any manual, webinar or workshop that tells you otherwise. Instead, ask any entrepreneur whether they are ever fully at ease, and they will tell you. But don't lose heart.

What you learn, though, over the years is that you can only worry for so long, literally: After a day or two of worrying that this will be the end of it all, the mind will tire of the wide-eyed despair and a lightness of being will set in that is nothing short of amazing. And it will kick in reliably, so wait for it before you do anything rash. It is the peace of mind that comes with despondency or actual loss. And it is not the only comfort.

I'm probably stating the obvious, but holed up in your office you can lose sight of it: You may not wish to come out at all but want to hide until whatever plagues you has passed. Especially men tend to shun human company during crises. Women tend to discuss their troubles with their best friends or partners, and so should you. Seek the comfort of a loved one, talk it all out, dissolve in tears, don't keep things pent up inside. Again, the freelance business follows cycles, and the seven lean years are always followed by seven fat ones. You need to force yourself to take the long-term view, and the best way to do so is to get your mind off the present situation by letting your lover pamper you, playing with your kids, hanging out with friends, but, in any case, having people around you, not bottles.

In a nut shell, you must take good care of your body, mind and spirit by creating safeguards and breaks, because only collectively will they function properly as the freelance translation business that stands and falls with you.

Try These Hacks

In closing, let me share some nuggets that do not merit chapters of their own but may be useful to you nonetheless, insights gained through frontline experience. They represent the very seeds of this chapbook because they are easily understood and easy to pass on and thus gave me the idea to start keeping notes. In fact, they might inspire you to write your own notebook of useful hacks. Their order is random, just so you know.

RECOMMENDING OTHER TRANSLATORS if you have to pass on an assignment is rarely a good idea. If you recommend someone or an agency whose quality you cannot vouch for, you may be rendering your client a disservice and it will not make you look better despite your superior performance because you are the one who made the recommendation. If you recommend someone you highly respect, there is no guarantee that your client will be happy with your colleague's work, since what is at issue is ultimately aesthetic taste.

Conversely, I have had colleagues ask me not to recommend their services anymore because they thought my clients too fussy. Occasionally, it will be a safe bet, depending on the client and the other translator, but suppose everything goes smooth as butter: The collaboration might give your client the idea to stick with your colleague rather than return to you next time. In which case you will be sore at both of them.

Instead, I refer clients I cannot accommodate to the homepage of the German Association of Interpreters and Translators (BDÜ) of which I, too, am a member, where they can use a search mask to find an expert by language pair and field.

COLLECTING RECEIVABLES is the bug bear par excellence for any freelancer, and the worst thing you can do is to get tough. You are not a corporation with clout and legal staff, and your threats carry no punch. Even a court-sent reminder will cost you money before any money is paid to you. I have found it most effective to whine and make myself a nuisance until whoever owes me pays my invoice just to have me off their back.

Throughout this carefully staged charade you must never lose your temper, but play the ingenue who bears no grudges. Inquire about the invoice by saying that they sometimes get lost in the mail (which does happen). During your next call, you apologise and consider the possibility that it has already been paid and just been overlooked by you (which does happen, too). Talk to the Accounting department one day and to your contact in Marketing the next, play one against another, a pesky but friendly nuisance. And hey: as often as not, it will turn out to be an oversight on your or their part, and almost never ill will.

The other day it turned out I had prepared a PDF invoice but forgotten to mail it. The buffoon act I used for my inquiry gave all of us a chance to have a good laugh about it, I got my money the same week, and no one lost face. The year before last, I only had to write off a single uncollected invoice, and none at all last year.

SKIPPING DIFFICULT PASSAGES in your translations has nothing to do with copping out but is an effective way to keep things flowing. Literally so, because like water you bypass an opaque line or paragraph and continue with a section of more transparent meaning. Chances are that it will cast light on the unclear section you skipped without costing you time to research things the text is about to explain anyway. By the same logic, you could put a difficult or tedious assignment on the back-burner und let yourself be tempted to work on something easier (which perhaps seems easy only because of the contrast and would have been equally pesky without it) before switching back to the tricky text. If you have trouble keeping up your motivation to translate in general, do some administrative stuff that you would normally be loath to do but that suddenly feels like a welcome distraction.

Staying productive by responding flexibly to fatigue or obstacles is much more satisfying than taking a non-productive break that will not rekindle your motivation or concentration. I used to play Pac-Man to deal with such roadblocks, only to realise that the frustration of the job was compounded by the humiliation of losing at an unwinnable game. If you do need a treat in between, set yourself little milestones that carry a reward: ten minutes of social media after you finish the current paragraph or page, a candy bar once you handed in the current rush job. I actually learned this from my children, and it works just as well with my adult self. To be perfectly honest: This very section was written as a reward for having completed the translation of a short newsletter, with the added benefit that the sweet larceny of work time to pursue this frolic of my own effectively eliminated any risk of writer's block.

BUILDING CUSHIONS INTO YOUR SCHEDULE will save you the embarrassment of having to ask for extra time if your work takes longer than you anticipated, while creating the opportunity to deliver early if your work proceeds as planned. The client's time permitting, I usually give myself an extra day, because you are only one rush job away from missing your deadline. Delivering ahead of schedule has never created problems or prompted clients to stop taking my estimated turnaround times seriously because this is not a game. They do need their texts, and the sooner the better. They are relieved they get it early without having to pay extra. In fact, delaying delivery just to make your scheduling seem more accurate may cause you to forget the delivery altogether. What if there was a power outage just as you get ready to send out your file at the promised delivery time? You would kick yourself, and rightly so.

TRYING TO DISCIPLINE YOUR CLIENT is not a good idea because you are forgetting your place. But the client's failure to submit open files can admittedly become so annoying that even I will charge extra for converting PDF files into a file format that can be processed or for excerpting entire homepages just to compile a quote. OCR software is a mixed bag insofar as it works with text boxes, some of which are not text at all.

And while CAT technology gets more sophisticated all the time, the point is that a freelance translator cannot normally provide desktop publishing and layout services like large agencies do.

Much more effective than applying a surcharge (which is a pittance for a corporate client anyway) is to say that having no open files will seriously delay the project. As often as not, the open files will be readily available in another department or at your client's own client. Personally, I dream of refusing such jobs flat out one day, but I'm not there yet.

KEEPING IMPECCABLE RECORDS will not only help you find things when you need them again but also turn you into a back-office archive of your client's. It happens from time to time that clients will ask timidly whether I still have a certain document they submitted ten years ago, and I usually do. Creating a filing system and method, rather than being pedantic, will actually save you and your client a lot of time. I have noted on occasion that clients adopted my filing system, and I'm not surprised because it is the easiest in the world (and not my idea at all): Put the date at the front of every file name in the pattern "yymmdd" and they will automatically be filed in chronological order.

RESEARCHING EVERY PHRASE AND NAME on the internet will not only make you sure you got your facts and figures right but will also make you a final proof reader for the client's copy. Especially if you have a lot of urgent press releases to translate, you will render a valuable service to your client by feeding errors and typos back to them. If your client finds a certain term or phrase unusual, all you have to do it tell him to do his own search and he will find the same things you found.

It has proven very helpful to me to run entire clauses through a search engine, specifying the target country, to see if I get a match. I will not use my translation if I get no hits, but rephrase it until I do. Complaints have steadily declined as a result. The drawback is that I spend more time on my assignments than I used to, causing me to lose money. But I feel better about my work—as do my clients, of course.

ACCEPTING BLAME when you deserve it will demonstrate your integrity and maturity. Even if you are not to blame, you will score in terms of accountability by helping your client sort things out, by looking forward and finding a viable solution rather than looking back to identify the culprit.

Being defensive is sure to erode your credibility, no matter what the facts of the matter are. Even if it is just for effect, consider the possibility that you may have caused something to go wrong or failed to do something to prevent it, or that you may have misunderstood or misinterpreted things. Partner with your client in addressing the issue and it will become an opportunity to bond.

In case you really are responsible, be generous in your effort to make up for your mistake. Let the client have the entire translation for free, charge nothing for extra work to revise it, promise a discount on the next job (and thereby give your client a reason to come back). Brief the client, where relevant, on steps you have taken to prevent similar mishaps in the future. Put yourself in your client's shoes and try to see things from the client side. A crisis overcome together might actually deepen your ties. I'm sure you get the idea: It's more or less the same in all walks of life.

DETAILING YOUR NEXT STEP in your email correspondence can save you a lot of misunderstandings. Not every client will clearly specify what is expected of you. The often used phrase "we need" or—hazier yet—"we would need" technically leaves it open to your interpretation whether you just got an assignment to complete or an inquiry for information, meaning a request for a quote. It has proven quite useful to begin my replies with phrases like "Thank you for your inquiry" or "Thank you for your order" because it will tell your client or team head immediately how you understood their mail. It gives them a chance to get back to you and clarify things, lest you start on a job you have not actually been awarded. Inversely, it cannot hurt to have the client confirm that you are to start on the assignment without further ado. To a novice, this may seem like another pedantic quirk, but experience has taught me that it is best not to assume anything.

Is there a theme that these and other nuggets from my bag of tricks share? Certainly so, but there is nothing tricky about it: common sense and common decency should govern this as any other trade, and getting things right the first time and without cutting corners tends to be the laziest approach of all because its efficiency makes it the least time-consuming one. As I said in my opening remarks, quoting one of my university teachers: Trust your senses.

Sources & Acknowledgments

While this chapbook is based on first-hand experience and uses no other sources, I'd like to recommend Douglas Robinson's seminal work *Becoming a Translator* (Routledge, 1997) to any kind of translator for further reading. Another useful manual specifically for freelance translators is *101 Things a Translator Needs to Know*, a collection of essays on the subject by various authors (WLF 101 Publishing, 2014).

Since this account of the freelance translator is itself a freelance effort assisted by no one, I need not acknowledge anything by anybody. However, it might make her day if I thank my wife for patiently putting up with this nonsense of writing a book during the Christmas holidays, and for sharing her thoughts on the first draft. And although it is sure to embarrass Silke Lühr-mann if I put my gratitude for her kind preface and advice into words, I shall, of course, do so anyway: Thank you both ever so much!

OTHER BOOKS BY
GEORGE GUILLEMIN
AVAILABLE FROM
EDITION CAFÉ DE NUIT

WHERE YOU BROUGHT ME
(short prose)

BONE CAMERA
(novel)

CARA Y CRUZ
(poetry)

MONOCHROME ROMANCE
(photography)

www.edition-cafe-de-nuit.com

.

37747553R00080

Printed in Poland
by Amazon Fulfillment
Poland Sp. z o.o., Wrocław